D1646758

BFI FILM CLAS

. . . .

Edward Busco
SERIES EDI

Colin MacCabe and David Meeker
SERIES CONSULTANTS

Cinema is a fragile medium. Many of the great classic films of the past now exist, if at all, in damaged or incomplete prints. Concerned about the deterioration in the physical state of our film heritage, the National Film and Television Archive, a Division of the British Film Institute, has compiled a list of 360 key films in the history of the cinema. The long-term goal of the Archive is to build a collection of perfect showprints of these films, which will then be screened regularly at the Museum of the Moving Image in London in a year-round repertory.

BFI Film Classics is a series of books commissioned to stand alongside these titles. Authors, including film critics and scholars, filmmakers, novelists, historians and those distinguished in the arts, have been invited to write on a film of their choice, drawn from the Archive's list. Each volume presents the author's own insights into the chosen film, together with a brief production history and a detailed filmography, notes and bibliography. The numerous illustrations have been specially made from the Archive's own prints.

With new titles published each year, the BFI Film Classics series will rapidly grow into an authoritative and highly readable guide to the great films of world cinema.

Could scarcely be improved upon ... informative, intelligent, jargon-free companions.
The Observer

Cannily but elegantly packaged BFI Classics will make for a neat addition to the most discerning shelves
New Statesman & Society

Programme of the première of *Napoléon* at the Paris Opéra

NAPOLÉON

·····················

Nelly Kaplan

ADAPTED AND COMPILED FROM
FRENCH ORIGINALS BY BERNARD McGUIRK

BFI PUBLISHING

First published in 1994 by the
BRITISH FILM INSTITUTE
21 Stephen Street, London W1P 1PL

The British Film Institute exists
to encourage the development of film, television
and video in the United Kingdom,
and to promote knowledge, understanding and
enjoyment of the culture of the moving image.
Its activities include the National Film and Television
Archive, the National Film Theatre;
the Museum of the Moving Image;
the London Film Festival; the production and
distribution of film and video; funding and support for
regional activities; Library and Information Services;
Stills, Posters and Designs; Research,
Publishing and Education; and the monthly
Sight and Sound magazine.

British Library Cataloguing-in-Publication Data
A catalogue record for this book is available
from the British Library

ISBN 0-85170-466-2

Designed by
Andrew Barron & Collis Clements Associates

Typesetting by
Fakenham Photosetting Limited, Norfolk

Printed in Great Britain by
The Trinity Press, Worcester

CONTENTS

LES VOYAGES ET LES EXPLOITS DU GRAND GENERAL BUONAPARTE EN DIVERS PAYS

FILMS ABEL GANCE · 8 · RUE RICHELIEU.

6   Letter-head of Abel Gance's Société des Films

ACKNOWLEDGMENTS

I have known Bernard McGuirk for some years, since the time I was looking for a creative collaborator to produce an English version of the script of my film *Plaisir d'Amour*. I was immediately attracted by his immense culture, his literary rigour and, last but not least, his devastating sense of humour. What began as a professional collaboration quickly became one of friendship and mutual respect. It is both an honour and a joy for me that someone of such wide-ranging gifts as Bernard McGuirk has agreed to translate my book on Abel Gance.

Nelly Kaplan

We also wish to thank Pam Attenborough of the University of Nottingham for her patience and expertise in preparing this volume for press.

All the pictures and documents reproduced in this book are from the private collection of Nelly Kaplan.

Abel Gance in the role of Saint-Just. Dedicated to Nelly Kaplan: 'Be daring, said Saint-Just – modern cinema, alas, doesn't know the meaning of the word! To Nelly Kaplan, ever daring, Abel Gance 1957'

PREFACE

....

There was once a film, rather many films, called *Napoléon*. Like Proteus, *Napoléon* was self-multiplying, in twenty or more versions. Like Penelope, a certain Abel Gance, its creator, was self-sacrificing, in countless visions, takes, retakes, cuts, recuts, re-editings, even burnt offerings (of despair). Work in progress...

'*If I had to live my life over again*,' he once said in an interview, '*it wouldn't be in films*', going on to the whys and wherefores of his having destroyed the triptychs of the famous Twin Tempest of the Assembly scenes. Yet, stronger than him as it was, the film turned irresistibly into an apotheosis as, for half a century, he couldn't leave it alone. Some critics, indeed, see *Napoléon* as the beginning of the end for Gance ... Like the Marquis de Sade (who turns up several times in the screenplay), he could also claim that it was not *his* way of thinking but that of other people which had cursed him with such a fate.

Irony of ironies, then, Abel Gance so often returned to his canvas that, just like Balzac's hero in *Le Chef d'Oeuvre Inconnu*, he rendered it unrecognisable. In the end, though, it was still Gance's film. So what right have I to judge his alterations? Though my own preference tends towards what is left of the first, 1927, version, both Gance and his *Napoléon* will always remain some way beyond us, forever out of reach.

A notebook from the log of *Napoléon*

I have chosen to discuss this film, these films, from the eye of the storm, as close as possible to the point of view of Gance himself – *Napoléon* as he wrote it, loved it, dreamed it. I shall leave to the film buffs the nit-picking comparison of the original and the restored versions which, undoubtedly made in good faith, could not avoid a degree of arbitrariness. Take, for instance, the old eye-witness who reconstructed from memory, more than fifty years on, the destroyed triptych of the Twin Tempest scene. Anyway, Gance wasn't there to protest, was he?

I must have seen *Napoléon* at least sixty times in all its different versions, and have been fortunate to have in my possession several drafts of the script, often quite at variance with each other. I've read hundreds of Gance's hand-written notes, pored over his diaries, perused a thousand stills, many of them from scenes either lost or unused. Above all, I have often been privileged to hear Gance's own retelling of the filming itself. All this has given me an exclusively personal vision of the film, the one I wish to capture in this book. I take it for granted that my readers have seen the film. If not, then drop everything and get to see it at once.

Just in case, and to refresh memories, before plunging into the Napoleonic maelstrom, here's a brief summary of the 1927 version of Gance's masterpiece.

Nelly Kaplan
Paris, 1994

RESUMÉ OF 'NAPOLÉON' (1925)
....

First period

PROLOGUE. NAPOLÉON'S YOUTH. BRIENNE (December 1783)
In Brienne, where he is a boarder at military college, his innate tactical awareness is developed and he makes both mortal enemies and the affectionate acquaintance of Tristan Fleuri, a refectory boy and a character who crops up throughout the film.

NINE YEARS LATER AT THE CLUB DES CORDELIERS (June 1792)
Bonaparte, Tristan Fleuri, Violine (his daughter) and his son Marcellin mix with the crowd as they enthusiastically sing the *Marseillaise*, the new national anthem. Robespierre, Marat, Danton and Saint-Just reign over the Assembly.

THE TUILERIES. VIOLINE. POZZO DI BORGO
Bonaparte and Tristan Fleuri's family share the same modest building as two other neighbours, the Corsicans Salicetti and Pozzo di Borgo, who dance attendance on Violine. She rejects them, secretly in love with Bonaparte. Vexed, Pozzo di Borgo denounces the young woman as an aristocrat. She is saved by her father.

Second period

BONAPARTE IN CORSICA (October 1792)
In Corsica, Bonaparte and his family, faithful partisans of France, are banished by old Paoli, nicknamed *père de la Patrie*, who advocates acceptance of English rule. Pursued, Napoléon escapes in a boat, using as a sail the French flag he has snatched from the town hall of Ajaccio, capital of Corsica.

THE TWIN TEMPEST
The Tempest rages about Bonaparte's vessel at the very moment the Girondins are sent to the scaffold, victims of the political storm unleashed in the Assembly. Exhausted, Bonaparte is picked up by the sailors of the very ship which is taking his family to France.

Third period

THE SIEGE OF TOULON

Against the opposition of the supporters of the Assembly, and having built up the discipline and fighting spirit of the troops, Bonaparte, second lieutenant of the artillery, attacks the garrison town of Toulon, fortified by the English, and captures it for the French. He meets up again with the family of Tristan Fleuri, who had taken refuge in the Midi.

AFTER THE CAPTURE OF TOULON

The delegates of the Assembly organise a Reign of Terror against the people of Toulon, accusing them of having aided the English. Salicetti, Bonaparte's enemy, has Violine taken off among the hostages who are to be shot. But she survives. (The sequence of the Toulon firing-squads remains lost to this day.)

Fourth period

BONAPARTE AND THE TERROR

Having refused command of the Paris fortress, Bonaparte is arrested. He meets Josephine, Viscountess of Beauharnais, imprisoned with him. They are both saved by an unknown civil servant of the Revolutionary Tribunal who has developed the knack of making files disappear ... by eating them! From time to time, Tristan Fleuri joins him at the table.

THE ASSASSINATION OF MARAT BY CHARLOTTE CORDAY

THERMIDOR

In their turn victims of the Terror, Robespierre and Saint-Just are arrested and led to the guillotine, in spite of the pleading of the latter, played by Gance himself. Violine goes to the Assembly, armed with a pistol, to kill the tyrant Robespierre, but fails.

VENDEMIAIRE

France is threatened by a royalist coalition. Barras appeals to Bonaparte to save the country.

Fifth period

JOSEPHINE DE BEAUHARNAIS

Bonaparte is now a famous general. He falls in love with Josephine and marries her just as Barras, under her influence, has named him commander of the French Army of Italy. He sets out to pursue his Destiny...

FAREWELL TO REVOLUTION

Bonaparte finds himself in the Assembly Chamber, which is deserted and silent. He is interrogated on his plans by the phantoms of the Revolution. He promises to fight for a Universal Republic.

Sixth period

THE DEPARTURE FOR THE ITALIAN CAMPAIGN

The young general has to impose his authority on an ill-equipped and disillusioned army. A subtitle captures the measure of his success: '*This ragged rabble would soon awaken with the spirit of the Great Army.*'

BEGGARS OF GLORY

Napoléon's dishevelled soldiers march on to glory led by the dreams of their leader and by the spirit of the Revolution.

PAROXYSMS
. . . .

Gance loved writing almost as much as he loved making films. From 1914, to our knowledge, he kept a series of *carnets intimes*, personal notebooks in which he confided his thoughts, his worries, his hopes and his gloomy view of mankind. It is revealing that the name Napoléon already appears a good ten years before the film project gets under way. He is fascinated by Napoléon's character because he was a '*paroxysm in his time just as his time was a paroxysm of history ...*' Add to that Gance's *own* paroxysm (he was fond of quoting André Breton's '*La beauté sera convulsive, ou ne sera pas*' – '*Beauty will be convulsive or there will be no beauty*') and it's easy to imagine the high-voltage physical and psychic atmosphere presiding over the conception, the writing, the filming, the editing and the release of *Napoléon*. No accident, either, that Antonin Artaud, who played the part of Marat in the film, dedicated a later book as follows: '*To Abel Gance, with whom I lived in* Napoléon *hours as scorching as the life of Héliogabale.*'

And, to underline the convulsive passion of the undertaking, here is the text of Gance's address to his crew on 24 June 1924:

PORTRAIT OF THE ARTIST AS A YOUNG GENERAL . . .

This is a film which must – and let no one underestimate the profundity of what I'm saying – a film which must allow us to enter the Temple of Art through the giant gates of History. An inexpressible anguish grips me at the thought that my will and my vital gift are as nothing if you do not bring me your unremitting devotion.

Thanks to you, we are about to relive the French Revolution and Empire . . . a unique task. In you, we must find the passion, the folly, the power, the expertise and the self-denial of the soldiers of Year Two. Personal initiative will be all. I want to feel, as I watch you, a swelling force sweeping away your last rational defences so that I can no longer tell the difference between your hearts and your red caps!

Fast, foolish, furious, gigantic, raucous, Homeric, punctuated by organ-pauses which will make the dreadful silences resound all the more – that is what will be dragged out of you by the runaway horse of the Revolution.

Gance (with megaphone on his head!)   Gance directing (with megaphone)

And then there will be one man who looks it in the face, who understands it, who wants to use it for the good of France and who, in a flash, leaps onto its back, seizes it by the reins and slowly masters it, turning it into the most miraculous instrument of glory...

It is up to you, then, to recreate the immortal figures of the Revolution and its death-rattles, the Empire and its giant shadows, the Great Army and its rays of glory.

The world's screens await you, my friends. From all of you, whatever your role or rank, leading actors, supporting actors, cameramen, scenery artists, electricians, props, everyone, and especially you, the unsung extras who have to rediscover the spirit of your ancestors to find in your hearts the unity and fearlessness which was France between 1792 and 1815, I ask, no, I demand, that you abandon petty, personal considerations and give me your total devotion. Only in this way will you serve and revere the already illustrious cause of the first art-form of the future, through the most formidable lesson in history.

Abel Gance

In Victor Hugo's words: '*Déjà Napoléon perçait sous Bonaparte*' ('*Already Napoléon was thrusting through Bonaparte*'). But let us return to the genesis of the film itself.

WRITING THE SCREENPLAY

Anyone examining the way Gance worked on his screenplays cannot fail to be arrested by the minute detail, the precision with which each scene is written, described, documented and dissected.

Although he alludes to writing the screenplay in his 1922 Notebooks (where he threatens to suspend work on *La Roue* if he doesn't get what he wants financially, and to take the opportunity to return to his work on *Napoléon* and *Christopher Columbus*), as well as in the note of 1923, dated 23 September, it isn't until June 1924 that he shuts himself up in the château of Fontainebleau, at the invitation of the Curator, the historian d'Esparbès, to tackle the writing of the script in what he describes as '*deep immersion*'. In his notes, he alerts himself to the need constantly to synthesise. '*Must cut more in the preparation, otherwise I'll end up with six films for each part. Beware. This is the greatest danger,*' he writes in 1924. (On the same page of this Notebook is to be found a jotting in Gance's hand, added in 1940. '*If only I'd followed my own advice. Alas, it was useless. My first film was already as long as three, and I was only at Arcole!*')

In fact, on the second page of the manuscript, is the following:

Titles of the seven films
I – *Vendémiaire*
II – *Arcole*
III – *The Pyramids*
IV – *Austerlitz*
V – *La Bérézina*
VI – *Waterloo*
VII – *Saint Helena*

True to habit, Gance's vision was '*too big*', even if his friend, the critic Louis Delluc, encouraged him '*never to cease thinking big*'. For *Napoléon* was to end with the departure of the French Army of Italy, in itself a titanic and miraculous achievement, considering the financial and practical difficulties which beset this extraordinary film.

Much later, in 1959, he would film *Austerlitz*, in unspeakable conditions, in an exhibition pavilion on the outskirts of Zagreb, though with an international cast ranging from Orson Welles (in the role of Robert Fulton), to Vittorio de Sica (Pope Pius VII), and including Leslie Caron, Claudia Cardinale, Michel Simon, Jean Marais, Martine Carol, and Pierre Mondy playing Napoléon. Undertaken at a time when international co-productions were the fashion, the filming occasionally took on aspects of vaudeville. But that, as one of Gance's friends, Rudyard Kipling, once said, is another story.

As for *Saint Helena*, it was Lupu Pick (the German director of *Saint Sylvester's Night*), who made the film in 1929, based on Gance's script. (We shall come across Pick again later, for Gance tested him, in 1925, for the part of Napoléon.) As we look closely at this period of the writing of *Napoléon*, Gance's notes, often jottings on tiny bits of paper, are clear in helping us understand, piecemeal, his creative method. Here are a few examples in which, very often, everything is considered to be of '*prime*' importance, '*indispensable*' and '*definitive*' . . .

Gance during the writing of *Napoléon*

PRIME AND DEFINITIVE
Above all else keep Napol. within the popular conception of him.
Don't lose him in academic detail.
Stay faithful to Raffet and Charlet.
Anecdotes and simplification.
It is the people who grasp history and the people don't go for Masson, but for the prints of Raffet and d'Esparbès, in order to understand its hero.

PRIME IMPORTANCE – 1924
For Napol.
Prime importance.
For the first time, the public should not be spectator as it always is when looking at paintings, but actor, as it is in life – suffer with the wounded, fight with the soldiers, be in command with the officers. It must be so wrapped up in the drama as to suggest collective involvement.
Think very often of the pleasure of the eye alone.
I am constantly forgetting it. Attention must be given a rest, and the pleasure of the eye be essential for that purpose.

For each film – Prime importance. *In the margin of each page.*
Divide in coloured pencil the periods into:
P. PATHOS – *Red pencil.*
S. SUMPTUOUSNESS – MAGNIFICENCE – THE EYE – *Blue pencil.*
M. MOVEMENT – *Green pencil.*
Indispensable. *Maintain radioactivity during the creation of* Napoléon. *Only write in such moments as these.*

There is Gance's 'radioactivity' and there is also the metaphysical, the hermetic dimension of his work. It would be difficult to grasp that work without knowing something of the passionate interest he had in hermetic literature.

To understand this, it is enough to look closely at his book *Prism*, published in 1930 by the *Nouvelle Revue Française*, not to mention his precious diaries and notes. Here he names certain '*anticipations of the cinema*', in the prophetic voices of Picatrix, an Arab doctor (highly respected by Rabelais, who christened him the Reverend Father as Devil) who wrote in 1250: '*The composition of images is a spirit in a body . . . As for images, the sages call them* Thelgam *or* Tetzavi, *which may be interpreted*

A note in Gance's hand from the screenplay: Stick closely to the popular conception of him . . . Don't lose him in academic detail. . . .

Gance's note: Think very often of the pleasure of the eye alone.

as violators, for everything the image does, it does by violence and in order to vanquish everything for which it is composed.' And Gance adds: '*And here we have Novalis, writing in 1810: "Visible music, properly speaking, is images, arabesques, models, ornaments . . . Visible objects are the expression of feelings . . . All matter is close to light, all action is close to seeing and every organ is close to the eye . . . Every image is an incantation. A spirit summoned is a spirit appearing."*'
And Gance adds this time: '*Is the cinema any different?*'

In a famous text, dating from the period of *Napoléon* ('The time of the image is come'), Gance condenses all his creative theories in often splendid lyrical flights. Here are some extracts, which he read to me himself in 1957, and which I kept on tape recordings, later to include them in my 1984 film *Abel Gance and His Napoléon.*

> *There are two sorts of music, the music of sound and the music of light which is none other than cinema itself; and it's the music of light which stands higher in the scale of vibrations . . . There is noise and there is music. There is cinema and there is the art of the cinema which has not yet created its neologism . . . Already, however, several Christopher Columbuses of light have emerged . . . All is or becomes possible. A drop of water, a drop of star . . . Cinema becomes an art of the alchemist from which we can expect the transmutation of all the other arts if we can only touch its heart: the heart, the metronome of cinema . . . Our Art requires a harsh law, demanding, rejecting what is pleasant or original at any price, neglecting virtuosity and the facile transposition of pictures . . .*
>
> *Another thing: reality is not enough. Cervantes says to Sancho Panza, through Don Quixote, these admirable words: 'That's life, alas, my friend, with the sole difference that is isn't the equal of the one we see in the theatre!' . . . Just as the reflection of fire on copper is more beautiful than fire itself, or the image of a mountain more beautiful in a mirror, the image of life is more lovely on screen than life itself . . . Not theatre, not the novel, but films. What's the difference? It's this. Cinema is not satisfied with evolution. It wants the sixth act of the five-act tragedy and the sequel to the psychological novel . . . The image only exists as representation of the power of its own creator . . . There's the secret that I think no critic has grasped . . . A great film? The gospel of tomorrow. A bridge of dreams cast from one age to another, the alchemist's Art,* Masterpiece *for the eye. The time of the Image is come!*

Such was the psychic realm which influenced Gance's thinking during the composition of the script, however retouched and reworked the later composition. We shall return at length to the different versions of the script, as we shall to the stunning virtuosity of those famous '*secret technical pages*' of which there was only one copy, jealously guarded by Gance himself.

For the moment, however, Gance was cloistered in Fontainebleau, in the palace built under François I which is now a Napoleonic museum. His notebooks reveal evidence of difficulty, anguish, external pressures, of jackals ready to pounce.

31 October 1924
They want to take advantage of my lateness to place sanctions on me ...
and they've had the cheek to take such a decision without seeing the state of
health I'm reduced to after the enormous task I've just finished ... Hasn't
it been decided that if by 15 November my third script isn't completed then
they'll start the directing without me?

7 November
Stupid obstacles and time lost in getting money owed on my monthly rent
payments, on the excuse that the rights of transfer of the house weren't
included ... Monsieur Bloch is proposing this evening to take back 1,000
francs per month, from January, from my payments.

9 November, Sunday
I've been working all day to finish off the second film. I'm writing the doll-
shadow scene and the last Assembly scene.
The doll-shadow scene referred to by Gance is Violine's adoration of Napoléon through the amplified shadow of a doll-figure of Bonaparte at the time of his marriage to Josephine.

16 November, Sunday
Morning spent working on Napoléon. *Tremendous difficulties.*
Swimming pool. Feeling ill. Afternoon, exhausted, struggling against
awful lumbago. No writing before six o'clock. [Blaise] *Cendrars coming*
for dinner. Our common misanthropy brings us together in past, present
and future.

19 November
Working quite well. Organising my Arcole plan. I don't know how I'll ever finish this film. Enormous difficulties to overcome.

There follows a series of notes suggesting that certain '*business partners*' are proving themselves to be dangerous enemies. Financial and personal problems become a frightening burden. By the beginning of December, it seems a degree of 'stand-off' has been achieved. Work resumes:

From 4 to 11 December, I have worked non-stop, almost night and day, and I'm finishing off the third script. I'm very satisfied. It will certainly be a triumph, but with pitfalls ahead!' He's not afraid of saying as much...

CASTING

Alongside writing the script, Gance was thinking seriously about the casting. And so (as his notebooks suggest), he carried out some tests, on 13 September 1924, with Albert Dieudonné, an actor with whom he had already made four films in 1915: *La Folie du Dr Tube, Le Périscope, Le Fou de la Falaise* and *L'Héroisme de Paddy* (subtitled *For England*). Gance doesn't seem all that enthusiastic. Laconic little jottings emphasise his state of perplexity: '*17 September: Projection of tests for comparison. Dieudonné – Mosjoukine* (Mosjoukine is, in fact, one of the available options) ... *19 September: Tests with Van Daele until 7 o'clock*' (Van Daele wouldn't get the part but was eventually to play Robespierre). '*Evening. Study Dieudonné's face.*' The same note is repeated on 20 September.

Still not convinced, Gance did some tests with Lupu Pick. The latter's portliness, however, hardly matched the 'hungry fox' image of the young Bonaparte. Exit, then, Lupu Pick, though he was to get his little revenge, several years later, himself filming *Saint Helena (Napoléon auf St. Helene)*, based on Gance's script.

Gance tried René Fauchois, the author of *Boudu sauvé des eaux*; Pierre Bonardi, a Corsican writer, later to become his production director in Ajaccio and whose name cropped up again in 1936 when José Corti Editions published his *Rituals of Voluptuousness*. Again

Dieudonné casting test

Moujoukine casting test

René Fauchon casting test

dissatisfied, Gance did further tests with Jean Chiappe, whose only previous contact with acting came from his job as Prefect of Police in Paris. Still unhappy, Gance thought of Charles Vanel, Sacha Guitry, and even of the poet Léon-Paul Fargue.

Albert Dieudonné was extremely worried by Gance's obvious reservations about him. He desperately wanted the role. So much did it matter to him that, to force the issue, the actor came up with a bizarre stratagem. Dressed up as Bonaparte, he appeared in the middle of the night at Fontainebleau. He asked the patently terrified guard to alert the director of his arrival. The old fellow obeyed and stammered out to Gance that Napoléon's ghost was waiting downstairs. Intrigued, Gance went to see what was going on and there he found, amid period decor and lit by the ghostly flickering of candles, a staggering likeness to Napoléon. That did the trick. On 4 November, Gance arranged make-up tests for Dieudonné. And he wrote in his diary: '*I've got the advance for Dieudonné.*'

The role of the child Bonaparte was given without the slightest hesitation to the young Russian actor Vladimir Roudenko. The part of Danton was to be played by the opera singer Alexandre Koubitzky. As for Marat, he would be reincarnated in the striking features of Antonin Artaud, the same Artaud who (in vain) aspired to the role of Novalic in *La Fin du Monde* in 1929. But Gance had saved this part for himself, just as he now took that of Saint-Just in *Napoléon*.

Saint-Just, one of the most ambiguous figures of the French Revolution, a sort of monstrous archangel equally capable of the worst bloodshed and tirades bordering on pure Romanticism, was also the author of a mediocre erotic poem in twenty cantos, *Organt*. Few readers, even scholars, are aware of the work today but the transformation of one of the poem's heroes, Sornit, into a donkey makes one suspect that Saint-Just had some acquaintance with literature: Apuleius, Shakespeare, Giordano Bruno, no doubt crossed his mind.

As he spoke, the gentle knight,
Felt his back bend, to his fright,
His soft skin turned hard and tight,
His ivory hands as dark as night.
His feet soon horny hooves became,
He sprouted tail and, next, a mane,

Albert Dieudonné as Bonaparte

Then ass's ears and pointed nose.
Poor Sornit, in this spellbound pose,
Your heart will always stay the same!
Yet when he starts to speak he brays
The castle echoes, drawbridge sways.

(*Organt*, Canto I, p. 12, Vatican Editions, 1789)

As for Gance, also a devotee of Apuleius, Shakespeare and Giordano Bruno, let there be no doubt that his literary preferences played a part in his casting himself as Saint-Just. Not to mention the latter's legendary good looks and the hint of androgyny to which Gance would not have been indifferent. Whatever, there is a case for pursuing, one day, the reasons for such a choice, just as in his opting for the part of the notably Christ-like Novalic in *La Fin du Monde*.

Gina Manès wins the part of Josephine. A debutante, Suzanne Charpentier, will play Violine, the young girl infatuated by Bonaparte but never daring to declare her love to him. Suzanne Charpentier is rechristened Annabella by Abel Gance in honour of Edgar Allan Poe's *Annabel Lee*, one of his favourite poems. In the film, she plays the daughter of Tristan Fleuri, the cook, a role given to Nicolas Koline, one of the many Russian émigrés living in France after the October Revolution. He could speak not a word of French, hardly a major drawback in a silent film. Completely devoted to the young Bonaparte, Tristan is impelled by fate to cross the path of Napoléon time and again, at Brienne, during the Paris Reign of Terror, at the siege of Toulon and even in the Army of Italy, where he turns up as a soldier. In a word, Tristan served Gance as a *leitmotif* character of the type that is found in almost all his films, a clown figure used to add zest, to produce laughter or on occasion drama, as in the Reign of Terror sequences. At once pathetic and touching, Tristan's character passes through a series of fruitless attempts to gain Bonaparte's attention. Napoléon, of course, completely ignores the lad who had virtually saved his life in the snowball fight at Brienne. Vain pursuit, like that of Gance, of the bastard child in search throughout his life of the recognition of a father.

There remains one dilemma in the casting. Who is to play the Marquis de Sade? Scenes involving him are fairly numerous in some unpublished versions of the script, and rumour has it that Conrad Veidt was in line for the part. There is, however, no actual proof of this, except for a stray jotting in one of Gance's notebooks: '*20 September – 4 o'clock. Saw the German actor Conrad* Weit *(sic).*' It is interesting to note that in one of the said sequences (lost, or simply never filmed), the Marquis de Sade crosses destinies with Violine, offering a possible explanation of the way the young girl is saved by Bonaparte himself from the claws of the Terror, a detail which, in the version of the film available today, looks like something of a red herring. But to that we shall return. ...

PREPARATIONS FOR FILMING

It is now early 1925. Preparations for filming have not exactly been sweetness and light. Relations between Gance and his bankers seem to have been fairly tempestuous and the notebooks betray irresolvable financial conflicts. Gance's relationship with his backers is simply chaotic. What's more, Gance still hesitates over the choice of artistic assistants. With some justification it was to such allies he would look for support. '*Up to 21 January, all kinds of preparation. Lots of disorder, owing to two films being shot in the studio and to the fact that my collaborators such as Feldman, Geftman, Volkoff aren't yet free. I've thought of Capellani, Cendrars ... I've rejected Genina. Dizzy.*'

Dizzy, indeed. On 25 January, his anguish bursts through: '*I'm feeling ever more isolated. I'll always be held responsible, whatever happens. There's no heart, no breadth of mind to support me. And they're ganging up on me. Money. So powerful ... They want three scripts, though two would do ... They've delayed me for months on end by sticking their noses in ... I suspect this wobbly arrangement won't last much longer.*' On 31 January, things look brighter: '*Volkoff's definitely made a good impression. We're organising the tasks. I started filming on Wednesday at 4.42 – the cameras are rolling!*'

In the end, as his friend Blaise Cendrars later writes to him, you don't ask Prometheus about the state of his liver – just for fire. And Gance has fire in abundance.

FIAT LUX

The cameras might well be rolling, but the filming of *Napoléon* was to be one of the most frantic and eventful in cinema history. At the beginning of 1925, the crew set off for Briançon to start filming the sequences from Bonaparte's youth at the military college at Brienne. There, in a kind of prologue, Gance sketched in one by one the key elements of his hero's destiny: his strategic genius, his fierce pride, his solitude, the hatred he inspired in mediocre contemporaries, all captured in moving or comic touches which confirm the close identification between Gance the creator and Napoléon the creature of his imagination.

What is most striking, in this early phase, in every shot, is a creative exuberance rarely attained later on. Gance tries to make the screen burst with images drawn from every device at his disposal, urging his cameramen to exploit all conceivable tricks. The camera has to march with the troops, gallop with the horses, slide with the sledge, drop, spin, somersault ... He even asks Simon Feldman, his technical director, to build him a camera which turns through 360 degrees and which can be operated from long distance, a kind of improvised crane, first ancestor of the highly sophisticated Dolly of today. Not content with that, he develops a technique of superimposed images for frantic action scenes such as the snowball battle or the dormitory pillow-fight.

'*I've got negatives of* Napoléon,' he said in one of his later interviews, '*in which there are as many as sixteen of these superimposed shots. ... I knew that from the fifth one on hardly any would show up at all but, as long as they were there, they had potential. Just as in music, when you've got fifty*

Filming the snowball sequence: Gance (circled), Kruger and Feldman on the sledge

instruments playing at once and you can't distinguish between them, it's the
organisation of the overall sound that matters. In the same way, these
superimpressions were organised by me.'

Gance goes even further. His ambition, for the film to leave an
indelible memory in its wake, is for the images to be chained together
not only vertically, one on top of the other, but also horizontally, linked
together in the same fraction of a second, with a view to achieving a
synthesis in which every particle would play a coherent role. He insists
on the simple fact that, whatever the importance of a one-off image,
nothing can equal the impact of an image-cluster, for no work of art has
ever better demonstrated its omnipotent hold on time and space. Thus
emerges the basis of Polyvision in the pillow-fight sequence (one
undoubtedly seen at the time by Jean Vigo, who took up the idea in *Zéro*
de conduite).

So much for form. As regards content, the following note by
Gance is sufficient proof of his concern.

> *When is the audience supposed to cry? I must mark each scene of the script*
> *in bold and in colour so that they all conform to one of these three moods:*
> R – *Rich texture*
> P – *Pathos*
> M – *Movement.*

Gance directing a scene with   Shooting in Corsica
pistol shots

3 0   Dieudonné and Gance shooting in Corsica

It was surely a letter P, in bold colour, that marked the last scene of the Brienne prologue in which young Napoléon weeps over his lost young eagle. For Gance's notes reveal that, in order to bring tears to the eyes of the boy Roudenko, he had an orchestra brought on to the set to play, for effect, Beethoven's *Moonlight Sonata*!

In April 1925, the crew disembarks in Corsica, causing a local sensation. And with reason: Napoléon, *their* Napoléon, is back...

Gance is totally committed to filming in the authentic historical setting. The passionate Corsicans, filled with curiosity, follow the crew wherever it goes, rendering the filming itself ever precarious, especially as technical innovations are still the order of the day. One smiles in admiration to think of Jules Kruger, the head cameraman, trying in such circumstances to manoeuvre his remarkable bicycle-mounted camera. And the same might be said of Simon Feldman, the technical director, overseeing the handling of another of Gance's famous gadgets, a forerunner of the Loumas [a type of camera crane] used today.

But back, now, to Gance's notebook:

8 April 1925
The sea looks rough, so I decided to go to the Sanguinaires islands at 2 o'clock. We hired a rowing boat and a motor-launch. They were frightened but we paid them well. We got there about 4. Did two or three
lovely scenes evoking Saint Helena and, as yet, not in the script. But I'll squeeze them in. The sea got choppy and, after an hour's work, Dieudonné refused to carry on and sulked off grumbling that he wouldn't do water scenes in such cold weather. I think the scenes we've shot will be splendid but I've caught cold and I've been feeling an awful bout of tonsillitis coming on all evening.
On the 9th, 10th and 11th I stayed in bed, high fever, food poisoning, tonsillitis.

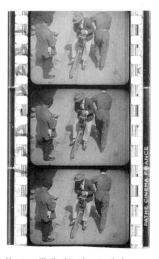

The notebook then jumps to 1 June. We learn that Gance isn't unduly unhappy with shooting thus far, despite the irritations of poor weather, an average of one good day in three, plus a bout of flu, a nervous depression,

Kruger with the bicycle-mounted camera

3 1

an accident involving Dieudonné and a horse. He writes: '*Besides, the fact that Dieudonné rode badly has proved a big influence on me.*' In fact, his great friend and inspiration Elie Faure, the writer and art theorist, had alerted Gance to something similar in a concerned letter: '*For goodness' sake, don't put Bonaparte on a horse Douglas Fairbanks-style!*' But of course, as everyone knows, great artists are horrified to think that anyone might influence them.

So, against wind and storm, he finished the shooting in Corsica on 31 May. Back in Paris, dark clouds are also gathering. Despite his personal energy, his indisputable magnetism and the exceptional quality of the sequences already shot, *Napoléon* demanded such a huge investment that it struggles to get off the ground. One by one, the backers are pulling out. His notebook reads pessimistically: '*21 June 1925. The* Napoléon *situation is very bad indeed. It boils down to this: Stinnes* [the backer] *crash ... Edmund and Hugo rivalry ... Becker, overwhelmed by events, gone overboard ... There was always something odd about the look in his right eye.*' (People will understand why, since the day I first read these lines, I've always looked carefully into the right eye of every new person I've met – N.K.) Filming is interrupted for several months for lack of funds. Eight thousand costumes, four thousand muskets, sixty

'Don't put Bonaparte on a horse Douglas Fairbanks-style!'

cannons, campaign forges, tents, flags, everything just gathers dust. Word has it that the film has come to a halt once and for all.

Little do people know either Gance's iron will or his motto – Leonardo da Vinci's *Hostinato Rigore*. By the end of 1925, *Napoléon* is back on the rails. But at a cost. Abel Gance has lost any financial control whatsoever over the production. Yet he is at the very peak of his creative genius and now films in the studio, frantically, the siege of Toulon, the birth of the *Marseillaise*, and the Twin Tempest of the Assembly scenes. He even forces himself to be polite to visitors, usually friends and relations of his backers, those set-invaders who have always been the bane of a director's life!

> *Every day I'm inundated by the world and its cousin, all eager to see me filming* Napoléon. *They usually come in smiling and babbling as if it were a music hall but go out looking serious and thoughtful, even pensive, as if some hidden god had just opened the Golden Gates to them. It is just that they've seen at close range how dramatic effects can be achieved, with more pain and suffering than we're led to believe in everyday life. There, reality can hardly compare to that of a studio where, with faith, one can create a veritable cathedral of light!*

3 4   Four of the cameramen assembled (Kruger far right)

It's as well that Gance can speak of faith and imagine the studio as a cathedral, for his notebooks are increasingly filled with his financial worries, often a sordid contrast to his flights of creativity.

Gance, one feels, is on the point of collapse. Like Bonaparte during the storm in his flimsy boat, he is hanging on for dear life to his film and to his script; he feels them flapping at the mast like the French Tricolour his hero had used as a sail. His credo, attached to the script every day during shooting, takes the form of the following confidential notes to himself:

TECHNIQUE
Director's Code – Personal
1926 – Always bear in mind
Absolute Conviction during the take.
Need très p.d.v. [*près de (la) vie/*close to life] *in all the pathos scenes.*
Don't get caught up in external detail in these scenes.
Maximum authority – Maximum naturalness –
better to exaggerate on this.

Don't get lost in details. Don't be afraid of pruning.
Don't be influenced by anyone. D.B.I.B.A. [In French, N.S.A.I.: *Ne subir aucune influence.*]

Before climaxes keep things simple.
N.S.A.I. Go for even more authenticity – closer to life.
Vary the shots for greater choice.
(This last note, incidentally, is crossed out in Gance's hand, perhaps in the awareness that any director worthy of the name should know instinctively which is the right shot.)

Always keep in mind above all: rhythm, length of respective shots.
More stress whenever pathos goes straight to the heart rather than the head.
Must be moved myself by the relevance to the shooting of the feelings evoked.

One of my grave faults. Overdoing things visually.
And above all mock everything. [We should not forget that one of Gance's favourite quotations was: '*Everything is tragic, nothing is serious.*'] *Essential. Follow my penchant, my nature, my own poetry.*

Suppress as much as possible the close-ups *– use them only when they're absolutely indispensable.*

Give more thought to the rhythm of the images, to their relative importance one to the other.

Sometimes do very delicate scenes as long shots.

Suppress to the maximum lighting effects so that those that remain stand out more.

Make use of a Carrelotti darkroom for the cameramen – Build one in the studio
Mechanically – get hold of skies – Brueghel –
Veronese (Calvary) etc ... blurred skies.

V.V.V.V. IMPORTANT

TECHNIQUE *1925*
Use as often as possible:
Du portatif
Vollensac
Eidoscope
Gazes successives
Fusil viseur
Brachiscope
Chariot
Cable
Giroscope
(Translator's note: Gance's original French is retained here since his techniques are often intriguingly personal.)

1926 – EXECUTION
Always remember:
The Swedes leave nothing to chance. The developments of a film are minutely controlled in advance – in expression if not in length – and their rigorous work schedules for shooting hardly ever let them fall for the seduction of an unplanned landscape or for any effect however admirable in itself but superfluous to the work as a whole. They therefore provide a useful working lesson. The Swedes master their rash flights and if they get carried away they always know where they're going to stop.

1. *Get someone to speak so that you can see what he is saying.*
2. *A conversation may be heard by a third party who doesn't speak himself.*
3. *Get the actor to talk from behind or in a three-quarter shot.*
4. *Show generally the person listening rather than the one speaking; the latter should be in blurred profile.*
5. *Use long shot, so no recognition of lip movement possible.*

These notes, written in 1925 and 1926, are often astonishing, even in the phase just before the cinema's entry into the era of talkies.

As for the question of whether Gance stuck to the letter of his own directives, the debate goes on. It is my own view that the motto N.S.A.I. (Don't be influenced by anyone), which crops up time and again in his writings, was one that he often applied even to himself.

. . . .

But if Gance has lost several battles his sole objective now is to win the war. In July 1926, Gance and his troops move to the south of France to film the famous scenes of the mobilisation of the Army of Italy. Here are the notes he writes to himself, which he is determined to follow:

> *Don't slow the rhythm after the address to the troops . . .*
> *Two hours later . . .*
> *The army on the march . . .*
> *Bonaparte gallops past . . .*
> *Beggars of glory . . .*
> *All the while, Bonaparte, first to reach the top of the Apennines, is lost in thought anticipating battles to come . . .*
> *The mountain-top . . .*
> *Italy! Italy!*
> *Battles*
> *March*
> *The Eagle*
> *End*

Yet while Gance finds the outline structure of his script useful, he is still ill at ease, like someone with his hands tied, constantly trying to slip his bonds. Then, suddenly, the idea strikes him: if he were to deploy one screen on the right and one screen on the left, extending the visual horizon, thus giving him three times the breadth of image, he could achieve a panoramic projection infinitely more powerful than any effect to be gained from distancing a simple image. (Three cameras, three projectors – Cinerama would be neither more nor less.) He asks for and gets from the engineer André Debrie the construction and delivery of three synchronised cameras required for the shooting he has in mind.

No doubt of the opinion that he hasn't gone far enough in his experimentation, Gance decides also to film these scenes with an additional camera, using the Berton process (which gives him relief and colour by stereoscope projection). The result is satisfying but Gance fears that the 'picturesque' impact of the relief and colour counteracts the aesthetic impact of the panoramic screen, and in the end he decides against using this addition. He is prudent enough, however, to apply for a patent for his invention: '*Invention patent: Obtainment procedure for artistic effects in cinema projection, Monsieur Abel Gance, resident of France. Application submitted 20 August 1926 at 14.41, Paris.*'

Prevention might well have been better than cure – but that didn't prevent Gance from spending long periods of his life in litigation over several of his inventions.

Gance's secret technique manuscript, 1927 (the triple screen)

THE THIRTEENTH LABOUR OF HERCULES
....

We now return to the notebooks. It is the beginning of 1927. '*3 January:
My images are taking on inordinate interest, at the cost of dramatic effect.
Cinema and drama are in a head-on clash, the cinema killing dramatic history at
every turn, just as music has progressively killed off the alliteration or
onomatopeia of primitive music.*' Three months prior to the scheduled
release of *Napoléon*, Abel Gance finds himself completely perplexed by
the miles of film which await him in the cutting room. Such was
Gance's thirteenth labour of Hercules – not only the editing but also the
need to reduce the whole to '*reasonable*' proportions. But what did
'*reasonable*' mean for Gance? How is he going to choose between scenes
which, for him, *all* seem indispensable? Now he slaves night and day,
with no respite. In front of him he keeps a single piece of paper which
he rereads at every sitting.

> *It's essential that I believe in the public's capacity to understand. Don't
> show too much: suggest. Keep it simple.* Let them do the thinking.
> *Don't pitch it at children. Make them detect the* invisible *in the visible:
> keep it* primitive.
> Be careful. Too many scenes. *Too much waste, not enough
> pathos, not enough condensed scenes.*

A month later Gance makes the following entry:

> *8 February 1927*
> *After the long editing process of* Napoléon, *I'm fully conscious that, before
> the premiere at the Opéra, I must shorten it still further, only leaving in the
> lyrical parts, the ones in which I assert myself most effectively:*
> *Snow fight*
> *Cordeliers*
> *Tempests Corsica and Assembly*
> *Toulon*
> *Phantoms of the Assembly*
> *Address to the Army of Italy*
> *Napoléon's soul*
> *Beggars of Glory.*

In another similar note, he underlines the importance of the sequences of *The Night of 10 August,* followed by a question mark. It is interesting to relate that question mark to a very moving letter from Elie Faure, dated April 1927, of which the following is an extract:

> *If you had the courage to concentrate the film on its great symphonic passages, its effectiveness, which is already formidable, would be tripled.*
>
> *I'm sorry that you didn't find it necessary to keep in certain sections,* The Night of 10 August, *for example, if I am to believe the programme photo, instead of several useless episodes which, apart from anything else, are incomprehensible to anyone who doesn't know the full script ... You have an extraordinary symphonic genius. You owe it to yourself to obey this fate. Lay the old song to rest.*

N.S.A.I. Gance did not lay the old song to rest, and certainly not the Violine story that had Elie Faure so worried. What is more, several episodes of *The Night of 10 August* were to be left out. (Perhaps including those, hitherto unpublished, which I reproduce later.)

On 8 March 1927, Gance confides in his notebook:

> *I've finished the long version of* Napoléon *on 37 reels and I must reduce it to 13 or 14. The criticisms go more or less like this: Duke d'Ayen:* 'In your place, I would cut the prologue and Josephine. As for the Tempest and for the Tempest triptych, frankly, they're insufferable and that's unanimous.'

Poor Duke d'Ayen was obviously sea-sick. Too much movement for him. Happily for us, however, Gance obeyed the N.S.A.I. motto.

'NAPOLÉON'S' 'AVATARS'

Napoléon opened at the Opéra de Paris on 7 April 1927, with its triptychs and with an original score by Arthur Honegger. It was an enormous success. To the enthusiasm of the public, the film was shown ten more times at the Opéra, still with the triptychs, but in a 'reduced' version of three and a quarter hours. A month later, another, longer version was shown in Paris, this time without the triptychs and in two

Gance with Arthur Honegger (rt), composer of the music

parts. Other versions followed, with or without the triptychs, and of differing lengths. Gance cuts, adds and recuts ...

Metro-Goldwyn-Mayer bought the film for the USA and re-edited it, making it incomprehensible. The result is catastrophic. Gance protests, flies into a rage, threatens law-suits. All in vain. Having lost all control of the production, there is nothing he can do to avoid the disaster.

Added to all this is Gance's conviction that the future of the wide screen and of Polyvision is assured. Polyvision, he is convinced, is to be a wholly new conception of cinema which will prompt a revolution in our way of seeing, our modes of expression in images and, consequently, our influence over the cinemagoer.

For Gance also wants to leave us a message. We read in his notebooks, in this regard:

> *Bonaparte was the French Revolution individualised, given direction, channelled, exchanging the guillotine for the sword. In this film, I have neither judged nor prejudged what was to happen to Bonaparte after the Italian campaign. Maybe after the 18th Brumaire I might have been among his detractors. My Bonaparte was in that long line of republican idealists of which Christ was the first example.*

And so his lassitude can be explained, as he realises that all the huge effort invested in the form and content of his masterpiece has led to an impasse. Thus, somewhere in the depths of his energies and sensibility, a chord snaps. From Saint-Moritz, in January 1928, he writes:

> IF I WANTED. *At the moment, I have all the possibilities of a magician in my art, the chance to change people's values. This means that tomorrow I can be Shakespeare, Perrault or Dante.*
>
> *Why then did I just smile and let useless flowers fall from my fingers? Am I afraid of the tremendous jolt my waking up will have on my animal nature?*

All these notes give more than a glimpse of the grave internal crisis Gance was in. He is returning to his obsessions with the laws of physics and the hidden secrets of metaphysics. He is reading Bacon, Albert le Grand, Ramon Llull. But also de Sade's *Juliette*. He is invaded by an overwhelming nostalgia for that poetic world which has been his and which seems to have abandoned him. In page after sad page he entreats the muses to return. He feels drained. On 28 February he brings up the need to gain a state of inner vibration, of generating his own energy, feeling an imperious need for '*psychic phosphorescence*'. Yet in May of the same year he is complaining again, in disabused tones, of being tired of '*bringing light to the blind*'. He is also plagued by the idea that thought should be self-sufficient. Why the need to speak it, to write it? He wants to give up.

In June that same year Gance was worrying, too, about the coming of talkies. '*Is man's powerlessness to exploit the silent cinema's potential about to burst forth?*' He was unconvinced by either colour or sound. '*1 July 1928. Stretching beyond the sphere of one's intelligence and sensitivity because of dissatisfaction with what is at hand . . . my engine is too heavy for my wings.*' Icarus is tired. We are in 1928 and morale is very very low. What was to happen subsequently?

Thereafter, and for half a century, while still making films '*not to live but in order not to die*', Abel Gance never ceases tampering with his *Napoléon*. Be it in 1934, when the film is given a soundtrack, in 1955 or in 1970, he cannot resist re-editing it, all the while adding scenes filmed for the occasion. Why did he do this, each time vandalising a little more his most successful creation? It is as if he wanted to punish the world for its lack of understanding, and for the despair into which the cinema has plunged him. Like an unhappy child, is he tearing the inside out of a favourite toy just to see how it works, or to capture the secret of its origin? We shall never know.

What we do know, on the other hand, is that Gance was never able to express fully, after *Napoléon*, his fabled creative genius. Prometheus has stolen fire once too often – and now he is exhausted.

SISYPHUS

. . . .

During our recorded interviews, in 1956 and 1957, Gance declared:

> *When you find yourself with a completed film, you are still far from having realised your dream. There is a loss of electric charge, of voltage . . . This cinema business, difficult as it is already, passes through so many*

hands, so many censurings, through so many people who have different habits from your own (and who, in general, are so minimally artistic) that you never find more than 20 to 25 per cent, at most, of the initial ideas you put on paper in moments of frenzy or inspiration . . . It's a pity, since I imagine that – with, say, a loss of 10 or 15 per cent – if one could make films as one would like, they would be so overwhelming that cinemagoers wouldn't be able to tear themselves out of their seats, they'd scream with joy, terror, enthusiasm.

Still, though you can't apply mathematics to this kind of calculation, I imagine I haven't reached 5 per cent of what I'm capable of. If only producers had grasped what I could have brought to the cinema or had had the slightest inkling of the brainless obstacles that were put in my path solely because I refused to be stuck in the status quo.

I wish tomorrow's cinema to be the true image for which it was invented, a school of exuberance, energy, grandeur, power, of the metamorphosis of man beyond himself. There are times when I regard my life as a vast deskful of lost dreams. And yet I always manage to react, for I know we must live out delirious fantasies, live perpetually in that intellectual exaltation which alone can jolt us out of that slow, so slow, biological rut of miserable evolution. We have to jump ever forward through hoops aflame with our own possibilities, never stopping at the dumbfounded sneering of bystanders. No matter how sublime the theatre or cinema we achieve, there will always be someone to listen, to watch, even if they are only that part of ourselves which we have left behind on the way.

In these words of Gance there may well be weariness, but he is never bitter. For he knows that the scenes of his *Napoléon* are incandescent. As Elie Faure put it, 'fire snatched from the depths of History'.

For Gance, then, tired and disenchanted, the years pass and he finally stops re-editing *Napoléon*, leaving to others the worries of tampering and retampering with his images. Abel Gance died, aged 92, during the night of 10–11 November 1981, anniversary of the signing of the Armistice of the 1914–18 war which had inspired his two versions of *J'Accuse*, in 1919 and 1938. But he was not one to sign an armistice with himself. And it pleases me to believe that, on certain nights of the full moon, he rises from sleep and, beneath the willows of the tiny cemetery of Auteuil, with an ancient Moritone, edits and re-edits a thousand and one times his *Napoléon*. And that, grouped around him, like the phantom shades of the Assembly, all his old technicians, actors and friends admiringly applaud the ceaselessly adjusted masterwork of the genius who for many will always remain one of the greatest visionaries of the Seventh Art.

GANCE'S INVENTIONS
. . . .

NAPOLÉON IN SOUND – 1934

Obeying a premonition, Abel Gance has ordered his actors, during the shooting of the original 1925 version of *Napoléon*, to speak the lines of the screenplay exactly as he had written them. It is therefore easy for him to synchronise the lip movements when he comes to add a soundtrack in 1934. Again, however, he can't return to the film without splicing in some new material shot specially for the new version.

The action is set in 1815. Supporters of the fallen Emperor, awaiting his return from Elba, are joined in clandestine reunion, evoking the glorious deeds of their idol. This effect is achieved by the trick of using scenes from the 1925 original, set in a kind of flashback, at the end of which it is announced that Napoléon has just disembarked, a prelude to the Hundred Days return and before his definitive exile on Saint Helena.

In this version, too, Gance uses for the first time his invention of Sound Perspective, as those who attended the new premiere at the Paramount cinema in 1935 were to discover.

THE TRIPLE SCREEN – POLYVISION

Abel Gance's vision of cinema demanded a screen of variable dimensions. Already in his first films he had sought, with his cameramen, ways of evading the constraints of that boring old rigid screen which, monotonously, proved incompatible with the ordered frenzy of his imagination. Only in 1926, however, during the shooting of *Napoléon*, does he find, as I have explained, the technical means required to explode the single image. To do so, Gance has recourse to two related solutions.

The first is one optical lens slid in front of another with a focus of 50mm curvature. The focus itself doesn't change, but the field of vision is augmented as if one is employing a lens of 18mm focus. The angle of shot thus becomes two and a half times wider and two and a half times higher. This lens is christened the Brachiscope.

The second decisive contribution is that of the engineer André Debrie who, at Abel Gance's request, invents an apparatus of shots with three synchronised cameras, the fields of which are added together, which consequently permits him to gain, via three equally synchronised projectors, a panoramic projection onto a screen three times wider than normal. Gance can thus execute his first panoramic shots on the historic date of 11 August 1926, during the outdoor filming in Toulon which captures the departure of the French Army of Italy.

For the premiere at the Paris Opéra in April 1927, the projection was pitched at 30 metres from a screen measuring 15.3 metres wide by 3.85 metres high. The projected image was hardly deformed at all, the angle of slope being 7 degrees. The lens, besides, allowed for the projection of three independent images, whether completely different, the same images but inverted, or one image of double width and the third one different again, and so on.

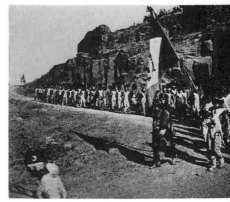

The three synchronised projectors were so regulated as to respect scrupulously the perfect continuity of the images when it came to using the panoramic screen. However, for the scenes in Polyvision the three images were separated by a tiny dark margin, obtained by a faint lateral decentring of the lens. It was not until 1956 that Gance was able to return to his idea of Polyvision, through a modest experimental programme called *Magirama*. In addition to the shots filmed for the occasion, a Polyvision version of the 1938 *J'Accuse* multiplied tenfold the wonderful and terrifying effects of certain sequences of the film, notably that of the return of the dead.

SOUND PERSPECTIVE

This was an invention aimed at broadening the possible use of sound and multiplying its sources by the intervention of different loud-speakers placed in the auditorium, spreading the sounds either together or selectively and allowing the spectator to gain a sensation of complete

The triple screen: the French Army of Italy in a single panoramic shot, and in a montage of shots

Gance with his invention of Sound Perspective

ubiquity. The soundtrack carries with it the commands necessary to unleash the effects of the loud-speakers either singly or as an ensemble. Stereophonics, neither more nor less. The patent, dated 10 May 1932, was applied for in the joint names of Abel Gance and André Debrie.

PICTOGRAPH – PICTOSCOPE

The process allows a freedom of expression in the cinema, not this time within the restricted limits of the traditional screen nor from the rigid concept of the association of words and image, but rather from the submission of the shot itself to real surroundings or to very heavy and complicated sets. The invention arises from the acknowledgment that the lens of the camera is not necessarily reduced to a single focal distance.

In focusing a mechanism which allows for the addition of different supplementary lenses, one can divide the field of vision into zones of different focal lengths. The focus being different, too, it becomes possible to have simultaneously clear focusing of both close-up *and* distant objects.

In this way, it is possible to record a real scene and, in the same take, a photographed or painted set, the dimensions of which are no greater than a few square centimetres or, again, a projected picture. The limitations of such a system are self-evident. The actors may move only within very reduced spaces, otherwise, any superimposition would let the set be seen through the characters. At Abel Gance's request, specialist television technicians developed an electronic system (the Pictoscope), combined with the lens-system already acquired by Gance's own Pictograph, in such a way that, with an image-mixer, the characters can move about freely against a mat black background and the image thus obtained is mixed with that of the set and filmed, at the same time, from photographs, drawings or projections. The economy of this procedure, through the possibilities it offers for being able to use all the sets one might need, seems obvious.

Gance incorporated the use of this invention into several of his films, such as *Louise* (1938), *Capitaine Fracasse* (1942) and *La Tour de Nesle* (1954). The invention, amazing though it was, was hardly taken up. At that time, perhaps, it allowed for *too* many economies! The enormous progress made since then by electronic effects has rendered it rather obsolete.

A patent application submitted by Abel Gance in 1926 was

Kruger (on ladder) and Feldman trying out one of Gance's inventions

headed '*Procedure for obtaining artistic effects in cinematic projections*' and was accompanied by his own sketches and detailed technical descriptions of projection and lighting effects for his wide-screen 'polygraphic' *Napoléon*. Patent no. 11.035 is therefore of considerable importance in the history of the cinema. [Henri Chrétien was an inventor of CinemaScope.]

Henri Chrétien
44 rue Tahere
St Cloud (S & O)

Dear Sir

31 August 1949

Monsieur Abel Gance
Chateauneuf de Grasse
(Alpes-Maritimes)

I acknowledge receipt of your letter of 25 August 1949 which has arrived here where I shall be for some time yet.

I'm sorry not to be able to be of some use to you in the making, and above all in the distribution, of the great film with which you are currently occupied.

I attach, as I promised you in Nice, a short notice on the *Hypergonar* which, although very old now, nonetheless remains worthwhile.

It's not the mass production of *hypergonars* for the projectors which would present difficulties, since the calculations, which are really long part of the task, are done for the anamorphic ratios × 2. There is theoretically nothing against increasing it to three times the range, but that, as I explained to you in Nice, would involve a long set of calculations which could not be undertaken and performed quickly unless I had, *a priori*, substantial financial resources.

One could in any case, with the existing *hypergonars* × 2 – if aesthetics demanded it – still cover the 3 × 12 size that you want. It would be enough to use, in the projection, shorter focus and concomitantly to reduce in height the projection window.

I am very touched by the interest you have kindly taken in the *Hypergonar*, which was inspired for me by the panoramic projections of Louis Lumière and by the showing of your great film *Napoléon* which I admired, at the time, at the Paris Opéra.

Please convey my respects to Madame Abel Gance.

Yours sincerely
Henri Chrétien

Gance's gloss

'I must reply and thank him and then, after making five copies of the letter, put it in the Triptych dossiers.'

LEAVES FROM SATAN'S BOOK . . .
. . . .

The following extracts from Gance's scripts of *Napoléon* are taken from the original Nelly Kaplan collection.

EXTRACTS FROM THE SCREENPLAY OF *NAPOLÉON*:
SCENES LOST, NOT FILMED, OR NOT INCLUDED IN THE FILM

A.   THE TOULON FIRING SQUADS (a sequence lost to this day: notes – technical secret)

787²   The commanding officer lowers his sabre.

787³   The 100 rifles are fired at the same time.
New technique (written in red on the original only).
I shall only say here that for the first time cinema will attempt to open up one of its new and magic horizons and that the

inexpressible emotion which will ensue, unprecedented in my view, from the fact that this new technique will not find its equivalent, in intensity, in any other art-form. I am determined to stress here at least the prime importance of the idea.

Gance's hand-written gloss:

787^A Shot of Violine. Camera turns, seems to focus on her in 10 images.

787^3 *Tech. exc.* The 100 rifles facing the camera lens resound all at once (100mm lens). And here, using an absolutely new technique, the camera will, to the end of this series of scenes, become the victim itself, and all the stages in the death agony will be played by the camera itself.

When the rifles fire, the camera suffers a terrible jolt and then begins to shake violently, while soldiers can still be seen shooting and others can be seen dropping their weapons and fleeing in panic; then a prism makes everything whirl, the pictures become first clear-cut and then flowing. All this while the camera drops little by little as the young girl [Violine] is falling to her knees.

The Toulon 'Fusillades' (The hostages lying shot)

There's a sudden flash and the terrified soldiers stretch out their hands as if begging pardon, then all is veiled; more images of Bonaparte; the speeded up dying of a flower, then Bonaparte again; all this happens in a whirl, only just, only just, another jolt, the camera is 30cm from the ground. The soldiers are seen to be advancing, their eyes full of compassion. The camera slowly, slowly slides down to the ground; the images get gradually smaller. On the ground another little jolt, then a final, fluid flash: flowers, Fleuri, Marcellin and Bonaparte, then a grey swirl, speed in all directions, then black punctuated by spiralling trails, then violet, then black cut by white for 2 metres only. We shan't have seen Violine for a second during this scene and yet we have witnessed every stage of her horror. What other art, in truth, apart from music, has the power of such possibilities?

Gance's hand-written glosses to paragraphs 1 and 2 of 787

Have Violine play this if the technique doesn't work as expected.

For Zette [one of Gance's collaborators]: have a cannon go off without warning her.

788   A cloud passes across the sun. Everything grows dark.

788²   Dining room of the convention members. *Icy cold. The glasses they clink together tremble in their hands.* Fréron puts cotton in his ears.

788³   A half-drunk Salicetti on the balcony of the window of the dining-room screaming: '*Let all who are still alive show themselves. The Republic forgives them!*'

789   Bonaparte takes his hat off to these dead bodies. He looks at what we cannot see.

Gance's hand-written gloss to 789:

The sun is hidden. Bonaparte is at the beginning of the wall behind the soldiers who have just been killing. He has little Marcellin in front of him. And he lifts Marcellin down. The sun is hidden. He hears Salicetti and leaps among the soldiers.

789²   The camera which was on the ground slowly rises to 30cm as if the wounded girl might benefit from this late reprieve, then to

50cm where we notice that she's not alone, that many of the wounded have risen up near her.

789³   Salicetti looking out from the balcony ... [*Gance's gloss*: sun hidden].

790   Violine is indeed getting up [*and in Gance's hand*: with almond blossom in her hair. The almond-tree will be broken (sun hidden)].

790²   Salicetti looks on sadistically and shouts:
Subtitle – 'Fire!' [*and in Gance's hand*: 'Aim!' (careful, sun hidden)].

790³   The 100 rifles are about to fire, but Bonaparte has jumped in front of them [*in Gance's hand*: on horseback if possible] and forces them to put up their guns [*gloss*: sun hidden].

791   Salicetti furious and 'les Conventionnels' at the window [*gloss*: sun hidden].

791²   Bonaparte shouting [*gloss*: sun hidden].
Subtitle – 'Is this the end of the world?'

791³   The terrified soldiers throw their rifles down and flee [*gloss*: sun hidden. *And in Gance's hand*: Film this sequence once with the hand-held camera, once tracking].

792   The soldiers rush madly back to the inn. They are confused, perturbed [*gloss*: sun hidden].

792²   'Les Conventionnels' drag out Salicetti, frothing at the mouth [*gloss*: sun hidden].

792³   They burst out in disarray [*gloss*: sun hidden].

793   Violine on her knees, as if coming back from the dead [*and in Gance's hand*: sun comes out. She has almond blossom in her hair].

793²   Gently, soldiers lift up Violine and the old man who were only slightly wounded. They seem mad. [*and in Gance's hand*: Marcellin rushes up to his sister. He weeps.]

For editing: (Note: this refers to the previous scene of the Toulon firing-squad)

Absolute simplicity. Very sentimental. No affectation.

Close-up Violine. Use the almond tree better, and use a camera to produce a series of shots filling the whole screen. Shadow of the horse clearer.

767   Violine sees her father who cannot see her.

767³   She bites her fists to stop herself shouting out. Her eyes fix on Bonaparte.

768²   Bonaparte is there, what else matters to her? She drinks in his image and her features relax.

769
inter   Joy of Violine. We are forgotten.

771³   800 hostages to be shot. She says nothing but her gaze falls on Bonaparte again...

772²   and two tears fall down her cheeks which don't move a muscle.

774³   Bonaparte refuses. Violine is tense.

776   Bonaparte moves off. Violine's eyes are out on stalks. He's her sole support as she faces death. She collapses in sobs, like a little child. Horse shadow.

777⁵   She hides from Salicetti.

778²   She realises that they're calling her. She cries gently, like a bubbling spring.

783²   Violine tries to go back among the hostages.

787ᴬ   Inexpressible fear of Violine, and the waggon scene.

789²   Violine stands up, as if returning from the dead. Almond blossom on her. Sun hidden.

793   Violine at the fountain. The sun comes out.

794³   Scene with Violine, Marcellin, Fleuri. *Beware*: Very much 'point of view'.

794⁴   General shot – sunlit. Violine, Marcellin, Fleuri, soldier. She is led away into a house in the background which opens up. The chickens pecking, the horse is still there. Very, very slow fade.

B.   EXTRACT FROM THE NIGHT OF 10 AUGUST SEQUENCE

Note: I know that the enormous task of the Assembly did not take place during the night of 10 August. I know that St-Just was not there, that Favière was not up to making the proposal that I have him make, but it was necessary to establish in a gripping abridgement several of the most important objectives of the Assembly from the outset, and psychological truth must, I think, broadly excuse the required historical inexactitudes.
        St-Just is glacial, Robespierre impassive, Couthon sarcastic and

the hideous Marat is himself; they are going to find expressions we did not know them capable of in order to lay the cornerstones of the new social cathedral. And this scale of idealism will be ascended by these powerful souls as the infernal round of butchery grows and grows [*and in Gance's hand*: and as Louis XVI slips progressively downwards].

585³   General shot of chamber. Robespierre, standing up, is about to speak. All listening. Close-up of Robespierre. He says: Subtitle: '*I propose the creation of a civil code.*' [*Gance's gloss*: one should feel that the Assembly is built on ruins, on blood. Red shadows fall across the table (do the inverse ceiling scene from the one I shot in the poverty sequence with scythes, etc.)].

585⁴   A circle, around a giant brazier. (Camera pivoting, speed 1.)

585⁴⁻²   [*In Gance's hand*: Louis XVI, who had been keeping his dignified bearing, now lowers his head.]

585⁵   General shot of chamber. St-Just gets up.

Standing in the background, Gance as Saint-Just. Underneath the original of this picture is an inscription by Gance: 'Yesterday the guillotine – today the atomic bomb. What would St Just do? To Nelly!'

585⁶   Close-up. He says:
          Subtitle: '*I propose that the State adopt orphans and invalids.*' [*And in Gance's gloss*: Very, very good. *Then, still in his hand-writing*:
585ᴬ   Assembly construction.
585ᴮ   Louis XVI slipping inexorably. Fall of royalty.
585ᶜ   Popular exaltation.
585ᴰ   Bonaparte examines the royal crown and meditates as he looks at the gathering.]
585⁷   Another informal circle (speed 2).
585⁷⁻² [*in Gance's hand*: Louis XVI even more prostrate].
585⁸   General shot of chamber. Couthon rises unsteadily in his barrow [*'barrow' crossed out, and in Gance's hand*: basket carried by a giant].
585⁹   Close-up Couthon. He says:
          Subtitle: '*. . . The creation of primary schools . . .*'
585¹⁰   Another circle (speed 3).
585¹⁰⁻² [*in Gance's hand*: Louis XVI's prostration ever greater].
585¹¹   General shot of the chamber. Danton rises and says:
585¹²   Close-up Danton
          Subtitle: '*. . . The suppression of the last privileges of birth . . .*'
585¹³   Another circle (speed 4).
585¹³⁻² [*in Gance's hand*: Prostration of Louis XVI gradually deeper and deeper].
585¹⁴   General shot of chamber. Monge rises.
585¹⁵   Close-up Monge. He says:
          Subtitle: '*. . . Creation of the decimal system . . .*'
585¹⁶   Favière rises and says:
          Subtitle: '*. . . of a Museum . . .*'
585¹⁷   St-Just rises and says:
          Subtitle: '*. . . and of a Polytechnic . . .*'

[*In the margin of these four scenes, Gance's gloss*:

          Very, very good. Essential to cut from here to Bonaparte the observer, standing still, looking at the 'royal crown'.]
585¹⁸   Wild circle again (speed 4).
585¹⁸⁻² [*in Gance's hand*: Louis XVI falls into a chair].
585¹⁹   General shot of chamber. Marat rises.
585²⁰   Close-up Marat, transfigured. He says:

Subtitle: '... *Creation of national hospitals* ...'

585²¹ One, two, three, four sinister circles at once.

585²² Louis XVI crushed, bent double [*and in Gance's hand*: head in hands].

607² Inside Louis XVI's office. Drunken revellers in the background. Sinister silence in foreground. A thief runs off with a huge clock. Bonaparte arrives, seen from behind, he turns round, looks dreamily, his eyes are drawn towards:

607³ something shining in the shadows, behind an upturned chair.

607⁴ He walks over and, bending down, picks up the sparkling object.

607⁵ It's the royal crown.

607⁶ Close-up of Bonaparte. His thoughts.

607⁷ He lets it fall back down to the ground.

607⁸ It breaks.

607⁹ Bonaparte lost in thought. Fade.

Juxtapose with Sade playing the organ at this juncture.

C.   EXTRACT FROM THE SCENE OF THE DEATH OF DANTON

The death is seen from the personal point of view of the guillotined head of Danton ...

He says to Samson.

Subtitle: '*You'll show my head to the people, it's well worth it!*'

Particular technique [this sequence was probably never filmed].

868 American shot Danton at the bottom of the fatal steps; the camera advances steadily. Danton's head occupies the whole shot; the camera advances as if it were going to go inside Danton's head and the camera becomes Danton.

The camera ascends the steps, looking to left and right, then arrives alongside the lunette of the guillotine, rapidly recoils, but only for an instant. Samson says a few words to the camera – Danton. 'Yes' the camera responds. Samson grabs hold of the camera which falls to its knees, then pulls it under the blade. The focus will still retain the perspective of Danton's eyes in all its shifts; at the last second, it glimpses a straw basket dripping with blood beneath it.

869 Close-up. Josephine turns her head with a scream.

869² Continuation of the basket-shot; the camera trembles, then a terrible blow hits the camera. A red veil with even redder trails – 95 images – then fall of the camera into the basket. The images recorded during this fall will be upside down as the head has been cut off; we shall pick out amid the swirl some tree branches which stand out against the guillotine.

A hand seizes the camera – head of Danton – snatches it from the basket and walks it up and down before the crowd. We shall thus see on the screen for eight seconds of agony this still living decapitated head and what it sees – A fantastic deformation of the watching crowd, then in sixteen images, the *Marseillaise* from the beginning of the film, the guillotined Robespierre, flags, stars, swirls, a flame, a red veil – simultaneously: black, red, black, red, black, red, 6 black, 2 red, 8 black, 1 red, 10 black, 1 red, completely black.

One of the giants of the revolution has fallen.

870 Close-up Josephine turning away with a scream.

870² [*In Gance's hand*: A spectator kisses an unknown woman who, sadistically, doesn't look away.]

871 Wide-angle. Impressive silence amid the group of 'la jeunesse dorée'. Josephine doesn't dare to look round.

872 A little child laughs, tugging the skirts of his terrified mother.

872² [*In Gance's hand*: Lucile Desmoulins sees (*her husband*) Camille guillotined. We follow the tragedy on her face.]

873 The blind man continues to mumble, oblivious to what is happening; his wretchedness is quite enough for him.

The Republic, as Stendhal puts it so well, is wounded to the bottom of its heart by Danton's death. Its agony is to last for six years, until the Eighteenth Brumaire.

D. SEQUENCE OF THE MARQUIS DE SADE PLAYING THE ORGAN [Filmed or not filmed? That is the question. And did Conrad Veidt play the Marquis de Sade?]

550 A young man pours a bottle of wine into a delicate chamber-pot and drinks from it. A woman kisses him out of admiration for this exploit.

551   The dancing is about to start, but stops short. A noise has been heard.

552   In the kitchens, they also stop and listen.

553   Murderers stop, robbers stop; they listen, suddenly overcome.

554   *Sans-culottes* listening at the door. The noise is coming from there. They open it gently and stay where they are; they see ...

555   ... the Chapel. The great organ. A man who seems to be lifted straight out of an Edgar Allan Poe short story, frightening, pale, his face drained, is playing the strange and terrifying 'Dies Irae' on the organ. [*Marginal gloss*: Get Schreck to play.]

556   The organ. Very close up. Score of the 'Dies Irae' open in front of him.
      His hand turns the page and his fingers leave a red print. Shot of his playing. The man touches the keys slowly and his red hands, blood-stained, leave brown marks on the ivory. A dead man's arm hangs limply above the keys on one side of the keyboard.

557   Great organ pipes. The tremendous rumbling of the heady and lugubrious voice is heard.

558   Different shots. To capture the chill. Ill-at-ease, remorseful feeling. The chapel is full of corpses, hanging over the balustrades or wedged between the wooden pews.

559   The *sans-culottes* move closer to the enigmatic player, not daring to make too much noise. One of them plucks up courage and asks:
      Subtitle: '*What are you doing here?*'

560   The organist raises eyes so strange and so awe-inspiring that the men stand petrified as if the Exterminating Angel of the Last Day were looking at them. He stops playing for a moment, solemn and terrifying.
      Subtitle: '*I'm burying Royalty!*'
      and he continues playing.

561   Close-up. One of the *sans-culottes* leans over to another and says:
      Screen: '*D'you know his name?*'

562   The other one says, '*No, do you? No! So what! ... Let's kill him. He's driving us crazy.*'
      They embark on their murderous intent when a woman runs up to them, pulls them aside and looks at him. She draws back in

terror dragging the *sans-culottes* with her and she says to them, trembling:

Subtitle: *'That's the Marquis de Sade!'*

They all fall back as if the Leper himself were playing the organ. She adds:

Subtitle: *'The frightful secretary of the Pikemen's section.'*

The aura of terror grows visibly around the famous Marquis.

563 Close-up of the score. (Text and music).

564 Close-up of de Sade, at once ecstatic and satanic, playing the organ. Withdraw into general shot of the chapel: the organ shining in the background. The *sans-culottes* rush out of the chapel.

Fading very slowly in red,
The eye focused on the organ.

564² [*In Gance's hand*: A view of de Sade. Follow the Jacouty Folies Bergère process of superimposing his face on the massacred bodies. (Exceptional technique)].

E. SEQUENCE OF VIOLINE IN THE CLAWS OF THE MARQUIS DE SADE, SAVED BY BONAPARTE

[This sequence, perhaps never filmed, at last explains how Violine was freed.]

686² Unbolting of the cell doors.

686³ Alarm of the prisoners.

687 The mob bursts in and grabs the first prisoner it chances on in the corridors; then, while some say their prayers, others stride, their eyes haggard, round the perimeter walls, like wild animals.

688 An old priest gives absolution. Violine cuts off a lock of her hair.

689 The moon slips across the sky. Panorama of the black flag.

690 People watching. The shadow of the door on them. A shriek. Drinking.

690² [*In Gance's hand*: Two lovers kiss violently against the wall].

691 A second prisoner is taken from the room where Violine is. It's the woman with her child. She is brutally separated from him and dragged away. She screams out dementedly. The Terror is at its height.

[*In the margin is the written instruction*: See the Louis Blanc illustration pp. 13 and 17].

Prisoners rush towards the window, leap onto the stall above, hoist themselves up, tug and jostle each other, wounded, torn to pieces, they fall back down. Have the cut-throats of the American shot flashed in huge close-up within 2 seconds, the hand-turned camera rushing at them.

692   Violine turns round like a madwoman, then digs her nails into the wall as if trying to tear it down. And the flower she is holding, a tiny sensitive plant, is going to die too. At least she will save that. She hides it in the little hole in the wall.

693   The black flag and panoramic shot of the moon drifting across the heavens behind light clouds.

694   Rue des Ballets gutters awash with feet and arms in bits and pieces; it bubbles with blood.

695   Close-up of Fleuri in pitiful despair, shouting '*Violine!*'

696   Close-up of Violine. Her father's cries tear her apart. She can take no more.

697   Long shot of the prison. She rushes in front of the cut-throats shouting: '*Kill me, kill me now... I can't bear to listen to this any longer! It's too much! Take me away.*' And she takes the place of a young boy they were dragging off. She's grabbed hold of, but she sees...

698   Her flower-pot is tipped over and is about to be trampled on.

699   American shot. She gains a superhuman strength. She breaks free, grabs the flower and runs back into the hands of the cut-throats, her flower held firmly against her breast, then she hands the lock of hair she had cut off previously to one of them, saying: '*For my father, Monsieur, I beg you!*' He looks at her, lights the hair with a torch and then uses it to light his pipe. She throws herself at him and tries to snatch him by the throat. She is grabbed violently and dragged off. The *sans-culottes* she attacked says:

Subtitle: '*Mamselle fairskin. I'm going to drink a glass of your blood!*'

700   Close-up of Fleuri full of foreboding. This time, he's sure, the door will open and it will be her, her... He can feel it, she's coming, she's on her way. He can't even cry out...

701   Corridor. Camera moves back as Violine is walking along. She has slowly plucked up courage. Camera stops; she keeps coming towards the camera. Her face is ecstatic.

702 The onlookers in chains, attentive.
Silence. The giant shadow of the door passes over the crowd.

703 Close-up of Fleuri; he lets out a heart-rending scream and tries to rush forward. He is held back.

704 The crowd doesn't move, still in the shadow of the door. Stupor. Paralysis. 'What's happening?...'

705 Close-up of Fleuri, unable to speak and looking delirious.

706 American shot of the Marquis de Sade, wielding a sledge-hammer as if in an abattoir. He doesn't move, as if thunder-struck by the admirably pure little face which is revealed to him. It is indeed Violine, but so very, very lovely, so ideally beautiful with her neckline torn and holding her little green plant against her bare breast. Unexpected things disarm even the most savage of men and this terrifying man doesn't dare strike her.

707 Close-up of the face of the Marquis whose eyes are looking down at the flower.

708 Close-up of the sensitive plant, the leaves of which close tight.

709 General shot of the restless crowd. Very rapid.

710 Huge close-up of Violine. All the disarming purity of a Botticelli.

711 The butcher from the other side of the door is about to strike. Sade holds his arm but shouting at the mob:
Subtitle: 'She's far too lovely to die!'

712 Close-up of Violine. She's seen her father. Joy floods over her. 'Now I can die!'

714 The mob screams 'To death! To death!' Sade tries to go to the defence of Violine. They begin to tug at her. Some defending her, some attacking her, but the latter are by far the more numerous and more powerful.

715 Arrival among the crowd of Elisa and Bonaparte, who appear from the rue des Pavés. They get to where the prisoners are chained. Elisa is terrified and hides her eyes. Bonaparte is about to go back and take his sister with him when he sees what's going on and waits.

716 Close-up of Fleuri, tears streaming down his cheeks and stammering:
Subtitle: 'Save her for me! Kill me instead. You're nothing but a pack of wolves!'

717 Bonaparte looks at him – and then at...

718 ... Violine being defended ever more weakly and about to have her throat slit by a particularly huge and bloodthirsty Marseillais.

719 Close-up of Bonaparte; in a second, he assesses what's going on. Decisively, he acts...

720 American shot. Despite Elisa holding him back, he plunges into the mob holding Violine.

721 American shot. Bonaparte arrives, breaking up the mob by force. He intervenes at the very moment they're going to put her to the sword.

He strikes such a posture of ease and authority that they all look at him in awe. He holds back the arm of the sword-wielder and says to him:

Subtitle: '*Man of the Midi, let's spare this poor wretch.*'

722 The swordsman looks at him and, frighteningly, demands:

Subtitle: '*And what about you, are you from the Midi?*'

723 Bonaparte replies:

Subtitle: '*Yes. I am!*'

724 Close-up of the three faces, the swordsman, Violine and Bonaparte. The unprecedented sense of humanity unleashed by

The camera placed on horseback. Gance is second from right

the young captain wins over the wretch. He lowers his sword and says to the people:

Subtitle: *'Let's spare her, friends!'*

The kneeling Violine never takes her eyes off Bonaparte. The secret of this scene and the saving of Violine (authentic as well – Ref. Masson, and *Avant la Gloire*, p. 262) must reside in the effective charm of Bonaparte and in his powerful command.

725 The people, capricious and feminine, does a volte-face and brusquely changes its mind and shouts: *'Spare her!'* and all want to be the first to shoulder in triumph the one they wanted to murder only seconds before.

(This psychology is very much that of the mob of the September massacres explained so exactly by Madame de Tourzel.)

725² [*In Gance's hand*: Violine is led off to the shop of the bird-seller at the corner. Contrast details of the little birds and the brutish revolutionaries.]

CREDITS

....

Napoléon

France
1927
Tinted and toned
French premiere
7 April 1927 (5,600 metres,
not definitive version but
with triptychs); 27 May
1927 (12,800 metres,
definitive version but
without triptychs)

Production company
Consortium Wengeroff-
Stinnes/Société Générale
de Films
Production manager
William Delafontaine
Studio manager
Michel Feldman
**Casting director/
production manager**
Louis Osmont
Financial administration
Edouard de Bersaucourt,
Noë Bloch
Production staff
Constantin Geftman,
Hoden, Komerovsky,
Georges Lampin,
Metchikoff, Pauly, Pironet
(also catering and
propmaster), Rufly,
Michel Scripnikoff

Director
Abel Gance
Chief technical director
Simon Feldman
Assistant directors
Henri Andréani, Pierre
Danis, Henry Krauss,
Anatole Litvak (short
period), Mario Nalpas,
Viacheslav Tourjansky,
Alexander Volkoff
Screenplay
Abel Gance
Chief cameraman
Jules Kruger
Cameramen
Fédor Bourgassoff, Paul
Briquet (triptychs), Léonce-
Henry Burel, Eyvinge,
Roger Hubert, Lucas,
Monniot, Jean-Pierre
Mundviller (Brienne/
Corsica), Emile Pierre
Editor
Marguerite Beaugé
Art directors
Alexandre Benois
(designer), Pierre
Schildknecht (chief art
director), Lochakoff (short
period), Jacouty, Meinhardt,
Pimenoff
**Script girl and M. Gance's
secretary**
Simone Surdieux
Negative cutting
Henriette Pinson
Special effects
W. Percy Day, Edward
Scholl, Eugen Schüfftan
(short period only), Wilky
Projection
Bonin
Stunt men and doubles
Pierre de Canolle,
Engeldorff, Robert Guilbert

Nurse
Mme Marthe Mélinot
Engineer for André Debrie
Maurice Dalotel
Stills
Desboutins, Gedovius,
Lipnitzki
Make-up
Wladimir Kwanine,
Boris de Fast
Armourer
Lemirt
Weapons supplier
Mauger
Explosives
Ruggieri
Wigs
Pontet-Vivant
Electricians
Albinet, Doublon, Graza
Costumes
Charmy, Sauvageau, Mme
Augris, Mme Neminsky
Joséphine's costumes
designed by Jeanne Lanvin
Costumes supplied by
Muelle et Souplet
Footwear supplied by
Galvin
Music
Accompaniment arranged
and special pieces composed
by Arthur Honegger
Stagiaires (trainees)
Jean Arroy, Jean Mitry,
Sacher Purnal
Distribution
Gaumont-Metro-Goldwyn
MGM
UFA

Alberty
J.-J. Rousseau/ Staff officer,
Toulon
Paul Amiot
Fouquier
Angeli
General Henriot
Robert de Ansorena
Captain Desaix
Antonin Artaud
Marat
Pierre Batcheff
General Hoche
Henri Baudin
Santo-Ricci
Beaulieu
Beaumarchais
Benedict
Cromwell
Alexandre Bernard
General Dugommier/ Collot
d'Herbois
Armand Bernard
Jean-Jean
Beuve
Guillotin/ Lomon
Blin
Calmelet
Roger Blum
Talma
Bonvallet
General Menou
Boudreau
La Fayette
Albert Bras
Monge
Daniel Burret
Young Robespierre
G. Cahuzac
Vicomte de Beauharnais
Caillard
Gasparin/ Ricord
Pierre de Canolle
Captain Marmont
Sylvio Caviccia
Lucien Bonaparte
Acho Chakatouny
Pozzo di Borgo

Roger Chantal
Jérôme Bonaparte
Léon Courtois
General Carteaux
Dacheux
General du Teil
Pierre Danis
Muiron
W. Percy Day
Admiral Hood
Jean Demerçay
Captain Suchet
Albert Dieudonné
Napoléon Bonaparte
Engeldorff
Laurent-Basse
Boris Fastovich-Kovanko
(Boris de Fast)
L'Oeil-Vert (Bonnet)
Guy Favière
Fouché
Fleury
Carnot
Serge Freddy-Karll
Marcellin Fleuri
Abel Gance
Louis de Saint-Just
Jean Gaudray
Tallien
Felix Guglielmi
Corsican shepherd
Robert Guilbert
Captain le Marois
Joe Hamman
The archer
Haziza
Member of Bonaparte family
Georges Hénin
Eugène de Beauharnais
Jean Henry
Sergeant Junot
Philippe Hériat
Salicetti
Jacquinet
Montesquieu
Nicolas Koline
Tristan Fleuri

Koubitzky
Danton
Henry Krauss
Moustache
Harry Krimer
Rouget de L'Isle
Georges Lampin
Joseph Bonaparte
Georges Leclercq
Dutheil
Raphaël Liévin
Fabre d'Eglantine
Lomon
Hérault de Séchelles
Martin
Voltaire
Mathillon
General Schérer
Ernest Maupin
Washington
Maxudian
Barras
Daniel Mendaille
Fréron
Metchikoff
Augereau
Genica Missirio
Captain Murat
Laurent Morlas
Staff officer
Fernand Rauzena
Louis Bonaparte
Régnier
Diderot
Joachim Renez
Favière
Emilien Richaud
Brissot
Roblin
Peccaduc
Philippe Rolla
General Masséna
Vladimir Roudenko
Napoléon as a boy
Jack Rye
General O'Hara

Saint-Allier
The painter, David
André Schérer
Ardèche volunteer
Edmond van Daële
Robespierre
Vaslin
Franklin
Vidal
Phélipeaux
Robert Vidalin
Camille Desmoulins
Viguier
Couthon
Raoul Villiers
Boissy d'Anglas/Staff officer
Vonelly
André Chénier
Jean d'Yd
La Bussière
Mlle Annabella
[Suzanne Charpentier]
Violine Fleuri
Suzanne Bianchetti
Marie-Antoinette
Eugénie Buffet
Laetitia Bonaparte
Carrie Carvalho
Mlle Lenormant
Florence Dalma
Mme Danton
Maryse Damia
La Marseillaise
Yvette Dieudonné
Elisa Bonaparte
Marguerite Gance
Charlotte Corday
Simone Genevois
Pauline Bonaparte
Pierette Lugan
Caroline Bonaparte
Gina Manès
Joséphine de Beauharnais
Noëlle Matô
Mme Marat
Francine Mussey
Lucile Desmoulins

Janine Pen
Hortense de Beauharnais
Georgette Sorelle
Madame Elisabeth
Andre Standard
Thérèsa Cabarrus/Mme Tallien
Mme Talma
Louise Gely
Mlle Thomassin
Madame Royale
Suzy Vernon
Madame Récamier

Jean Arroy
Sans-culotte at Toulon/ Member of Convention
M. Pérès, Pierre Ferval, Edmond Gréville, Michel Zahar, de Bourgival
Friars
Florquet, Robert Arnoux
Convention
André Cerf, Francis
Soldiers

With Wells, Médus, Jean Mitry, Jean Dréville, Maggy Pironet

'Heartfelt thanks to the following, for their valuable assistance in the making of *Napoléon*: Duchesse d'Ayen, Princesse Edmond de Polignac, Comtesse Charles de Polignac, Mlle S. Guggenheim, Comte de Chevigne, Comte Jean de Polignac, Duc de Gramont, Baron Paul de Thoisy, Baron Foy, MM la Caze, Marcus and Arthur Loew, Léon Gaumont, Rubin, E. Costil, Ludwig Lawrence, Dr Brausback, Rudolph Becker, Paul Brunet, Antonio Mosco, Luchaire, Georges d'Esparbès, Elie Faure, Pierre Roché, René Délange, N. Bloch, André Debrie, Michel Feldman, H. Nièpce, Frederix – and also to those who, by their understanding, their assistance and their work, have added a building block to the construction of the film.' – A. G.

Print made from material restored by Kevin Brownlow in collaboration with the National Film and Television Archive. The above credits were compiled largely from Kevin Brownlow's book on *Napoléon* and checked by Markku Salmi.

BIBLIOGRAPHY

Principal texts by Abel Gance

Prisme (Paris: Editions de la N.R.F., Gallimard, 1930).

Le temps de l'image est venu (Paris: 'L'art cinématographique' collection, editor Félix Alcan, 1926).

'Les nouveaux chapitres de notre syntaxe', *Cahiers du Cinéma*, October 1953.

'Départ vers la polyvision', *Cahiers du Cinéma*, December 1954.

'Entretien avec Jacques Rivette et François Truffaut', *Cahiers du Cinéma*, January 1955.

'Le temps de l'image éclatée', postscript to Sophie Daria, *Abel Gance, hier et demain* (Editions de La Palatine, 1959).

Presentation and commentary for the film *Louis Lumière* by Paul Paviot (1954).

Scripts

J'Accuse! (La Lampe merveilleuse, 1922).

Napoléon vu par Abel Gance, I, Bonaparte (Plon, 1927).

La Roue ('Cinéma-Bibliothèque', Tallandier, 1930).

La Fin du Monde ('Cinéma-Bibliothèque', Tallandier, 1931).

Books and articles about Gance

Canudo, Ricciotto. *'La Roue' d'Abel Gance* (Paris: Editions Ferenczi, 1923).

Arroy, Jean. *En tournant 'Napoléon' avec Abel Gance* (Paris: La Renaissance du Livre, 1927).

Epstein, Jean. 'Abel Gance', *Photo-Ciné*, 1927.

Jeanne, René. *'Napoléon' vu par Abel Gance* (Paris: Editions J. Tallandier, 1927).

Scize, Pierre. *La seconde jeunesse de Bonaparte* (Paris: 'Oeuvres libres', Arthème Fayard, 1927).

Friedrich, Evy. *Remarques sur Abel Gance* (Luxembourg: Le film Luxembourgeois, 1931).

Gilbert, O. P. *La roue* (Paris: Plon, 1956).

L'Ecran. 'Abel Gance', special issue, April–May 1958.

Daria, Sophie. *Abel Gance, hier et demain* (Paris/Geneva: Editions La Palatine, 1959).

Kaplan, Nelly. 'Manifeste d'un art nouveau: la Polyvision', *Caractères* (Paris), 1955.

Kaplan, Nelly. *Le Sunlight d'Austerlitz* (Paris: Plon, 1960).

Icart, Roger. *Abel Gance* (Toulouse: Publications de l'Institut pédagogique national sous l'égide du Centre régional de Documentation pédagogique de L'Académie de Toulouse, 1960).

Kaplan, Nelly. *Dossiers du Cinéma III*. (Casterman, 1974).

Kramer, Steven Philip and Welsh, James Michael. *Abel Gance* (Boston: Twayne, 1978).

Brownlow, Kevin. *Napoleon* (London: Jonathan Cape, 1983).

Icart, Roger. *Abel Gance* (L'Age d'Homme, 1983).

King, Norman. *Abel Gance* (London: British Film Institute, 1984).

'Archives d'un Visionnaire', catalogue of the Nelly Kaplan collection, sale at Hôtel Drouot, Paris, 3 March 1993.

Films on Gance

Abel Gance, Hier et Demain, Nelly Kaplan, 1963.

Abel Gance: The Charm of Dynamite, Kevin Brownlow, 1968.

Abel Gance et son Napoléon, Nelly Kaplan, 1984.

ALSO PUBLISHED

**If you would like further information
about future BFI Film Classics or
about other books on film, media and
popular culture from BFI Publishing,
please write to:**

**BFI Film Classics
British Film Institute
21 Stephen Street
London
W1P 1PL**